On Cloud Nine

On Cloud Nine

(AN INSPIRING TALE)

Weathering the Challenge of Many Generations in the Workplace

**Robert W. Wendover
and Terrence L. Gargiulo**

Illustrations by Eldon Dedini

AMACOM
American Management Association
New York • Atlanta • Brussels • Chicago • Mexico City
San Francisco • Shanghai • Tokyo • Toronto • Washington, D. C.

Special discounts on bulk quantities of AMACOM books are available to corporations, professional associations, and other organizations. For details, contact Special Sales Department, AMACOM, a division of American Management Association, 1601 Broadway, New York, NY 10019.
Tel.: 212-903-8316. Fax: 212-903-8083.
Web site: www.amacombooks.org

This publication is designed to provide accurate and authoritative information in regard to the subject matter covered. It is sold with the understanding that the publisher is not engaged in rendering legal, accounting, or other professional service. If legal advice or other expert assistance is required, the services of a competent professional person should be sought.

LIBRARY OF CONGRESS CATALOGING-IN-PUBLICATION DATA
Wendover, Robert W.
On cloud nine : weathering the challenge of many generations in the workplace / Robert W. Wendover and Terrence L. Gargiulo ; illustrations by Eldon Dedini.
    p. cm.
  Includes index.
  ISBN 0-8144-0878-8
  1. Organizational change. 2. Corporate culture. 3. Conflict of generations. I. Gargiulo, Terrence L., 1968- II. Title.
  HD58.8.O5 2006
  658.4'06--dc22
                                                          2005021051

Printing number

10 9 8 7 6 5 4 3 2 1

BOB

*To Erin and Katie, the loves of my life
and the forefront of a new generation.*

TERRENCE

*For my son, Gabriel,
may your heart soar in the clouds
and give you strength
to weather any storm life may bring you.*

Contents

Acknowledgments   ix

Part I

A Story of Generational Conflict and Resolution

Chapter One. Taking Charge   3

Chapter Two. Survey Madness   11

Chapter Three. Seventy-Two Hours   19

Chapter Four. A Call to the Summit   25

Chapter Five. Mama Chom   33

Chapter Six. Wait Five Minutes   41

Chapter Seven. Puff, Huff, and Stuff   51

Chapter Eight. "Weather" You Like It or Not   57

Chapter Nine. The Dawn of the World Wide
Weather Network   71

Chapter Ten. On Cloud Nine   91

Part II

From Fable into Practice

Chapter Eleven. What We Can Learn from
the Story   101

Chapter Twelve. Questions for Thought and
Discussion   111

Chapter Thirteen. A Quiz for the Reader   117

Chapter Fourteen. Frequently Asked Questions
and Answers About Generational Differences   121

Index   139

About the Authors   143

For More Information   145

Acknowledgments

This fable was a pure joy to write and a gift from our imaginations to yours. Lots of people have been instrumental in the publishing of this book. Adrienne Hickey and Ellen Kadin at AMACOM brought together two unlikely authors. Adrienne's vision, conviction, and professionalism have driven the success of the project from start to finish. The creative touches of Cathleen Ouderkirk and Andy Ambraziejus have graced this book with its delightful look and feel. The AMACOM publishing team has been superb and a pleasure to work with. We are indebted to Eldon Dedini for his one-of-a-kind art that brings the fable's characters alive. Our families tirelessly give us their love and support. We know we can be a bit crazy when we are in the throes of pursuing our dreams and using our gifts, so we cannot thank you enough for being patient with us. Lastly we want to thank the weather and the clouds. They have become our dear friends; we hope you, like us, will never look at them the same way again.

On Cloud Nine

Part I

*A Story of Generational
Conflict and Resolution*

CHAPTER ONE

Taking Charge

Wally pinned on his shiny new name badge and smiled at himself in the mirror. He looked good, no doubt about it. Who would have ever dreamed that he would be appointed as the new Director of the Weather Customer Satisfaction Bureau (WCSB)? Barely two years out of meteorology school, he had landed one of the most prestigious and highly sought-after jobs in the weather industry. Wally was walking on Cloud Nine, and nothing was going to get in his way.

So what if all of his predecessors had failed? Besides they were "old school" directors. What did they know about today's hip customers? Old ways and old thinking were not part of his grand plan. Wally glanced at his watch. He had better hurry. He didn't want to be late for his meeting with Jerome Numberman.

Wally galloped into Jerome Numberman's office. Jerome had been working as a statistician for the Weather Customer Satisfaction Bureau for more than thirty years. He had seen a little bit of everything. However, the young, plump, rotund face of Wally with its sparkling white teeth and beaming smile was unlike any other he had ever encountered. Wally had a zest for life rarely seen in the meteorology business. Jerome felt tired just looking at him.

Wally's eyes widened as he scanned the posh interior of Jerome's office. The walls were decorated with colorful maps of exotic places around the world, and the extensive collection of degrees and certifications was housed in sterling silver frames. Jerome's mahogany desk was piled a mile high with reports. A typewriter sat prominently in the middle. "That's strange," thought Wally, "I wonder where Jerome keeps his computer?"

With one more scan of the room, Wally answered his own question. Tucked away in the back-most corner of the room were the pieces of one of the WCSB's state-of-the-art computer systems. Considering the shambles made of the parts, Wally was left with the impression that someone had gotten into a fight with it—and the computer had lost.

Wally halted his musings, locked eyes with Jerome, and shot him one of his trademark ear-to-ear grins: "Sure is a pleasure to meet you, sir!"

"Come in, Wally, take a seat, it's nice to meet you too," Jerome grumbled. "Now about the survey you sent me...."

Wally selected a chair and plopped himself down. "Great weather we're having today, huh? Should be like this every day. But then maybe we would be out of a job if it was," he laughed.

Jerome remained silent for a moment and then continued. "Listen, Wally, about the survey you've written."

Wally sat up straight in his seat. "A stroke of brilliance if you ask me. I thought you'd like it. From the research I did yesterday afternoon on the WCSB computer system, we have never conducted a customer satisfaction survey before. How could you guys be in business for so long and never have conducted a survey? It doesn't make a lot of sense to me. They taught us in meteorology school to collect as much data as possible. Given your brilliance as a numbers guy, I'm sure you concur with my thinking here."

The veins in Jerome's neck started to swell, and a bright red hue of controlled agitation was beginning to transform his stern, spectacled face. "First of all, Wally, if you had bothered to speak with anyone, rather than rely on those preposterous computers you kids are wedded to, you would have learned that the WCSB has actually conducted numerous surveys in the past, and that they've created more problems than they have solved. Surveys get people riled up. It's not how we do things around here. I remember when…"

Wally waved his finger back and forth in the air and interrupted Jerome in mid-sentence. "Now, Jerome,

Jerome and Wally don't see things the same way.

times are different. You guys are stuck in your ways. This is what we need to do. It's modern thinking."

Jerome took off his glasses and shook his head in disgust. "Measuring global attitudes about people's satisfaction with the weather is futile. Your survey is riddled with errors and will not yield any statistically significant data."

Wally mustered his best imitation of an air of authority and retorted, "Well, Jerome, we will have to let the results speak for themselves. I'm in charge here and I will send out this survey with or without your help." Wally rose from his chair and headed toward the door; motioning toward the heap of technology on the floor, he said, "By the way, if you want any help with your computer I would be happy to come by sometime and give you a hand." The last thing Jerome saw was Wally's infectious smile.

CHAPTER TWO

Survey Madness

Wally sat in his office daydreaming about the survey results. Soon he would know the thoughts and opinions of billions of people on the planet. The power to enact real change would be in his hands. Wally fingered the keys of his computer's keyboard absentmindedly, thinking about how to compose an e-mail to the WCSB Board of Directors. They would want to know about the survey. He knew they would be impressed by his vision. At this rate he could become president of the organization in no time at all. Wally then wrote the following e-mail:

FROM: *Wally—Director of WCSB*

TO: *Board of Directors*

SUBJECT: *Customer Satisfaction Survey*

Dear Sirs and Madams:

As new Director of the WCSB, I have taken decisive action to ensure the future success of our organization. As you know, customer satisfaction is essential to our ongoing reputation. I know you will join me in celebrating once we have received the input from people around the world.

While I realize there are some reservations within the Statistical Center, I have designed and sent out a survey intended to measure people's satisfaction with the weather. Forthcoming results will be forwarded to you as soon as they are available.

Sincerely,

Wally

Wally hit the Send button on his computer and did a little jig around his office. This survey was going to be his legacy.

Two weeks later Wally sat in his office daydreaming. He did not hear the mail clerk enter and drop a huge package on his desk. Reluctant to interrupt Wally's reverie, the mail clerk said in an almost imperceptible mousy voice, "Excuse me, sir. I think the results of the survey you have been waiting for have arrived."

The word "survey" roused Wally out of his trance. Without thinking, Wally said to the mail clerk, "These results, my lad, are history, and today you are part of that history. Generations to come will remember this day...." Wally was getting all wound up and was ready to launch into a full-blown speech. However, seeing the rolling eyes of the mail clerk, he truncated his speech in mid-sentence.

Toning down his mounting bravado, Wally said, "Do me a favor and bring the survey results to the duplication department and instruct them to make a copy for all the members of the Executive Team. Oh, and would you please be sure Jerome Numberman gets a copy as well? Then return the originals to me for my review. In the meantime I am going out to celebrate." As Wally skipped out of his office, shooting the mail clerk a broad smile, he did not hear the mail clerk say softly, "But sir, I'm not sure if you really want to...." Wally was already out of sight, and the mail clerk had no choice but to fulfill Wally's request.

CHAPTER THREE

Seventy-Two Hours

After a suitable celebration and a good night of sleep, Wally could not wait to get to the office the next morning. He was quite certain that members of the Executive Team would be waiting outside his office to congratulate him and ask him for his ideas on the next steps. He had prepared a response that he felt had the right mix of sincerity, humility, and oomph.

As Wally had suspected, Chiesel Gordon, president of the WCSB and head of the Executive Team, was standing outside his office waiting for him. Wally waltzed toward Chiesel and beamed a wide smile. But there was nothing inviting or celebratory about Chiesel's demeanor. The man's old angular face was carved by years of internal battles and tests of time. He was clearly not amused.

Chiesel went on the attack, and in a booming voice that could be heard for miles screamed, "Young man, what in the world possessed you to send out this idiotic survey? You have committed a reckless act of madness. The phones are ringing non-stop and everyone is up in arms over the disastrous results of this survey. According to our customers, our services stink. Over 90 percent of the respondents are completely dissatisfied with the weather. What were you thinking? Any imbecile knows that the public will never be satisfied with the weather; it's a no-win situation. The results of this survey are disastrous. You have done nothing less than jeopardize this entire organization and undermine all the years of work I and others have done to build it."

Wally's entire body started shaking with fear and emotions of every kind. Through tears and a thick fog of confusion Wally did his best to respond, "But sir, you put me in charge of this bureau. I did what I thought was best. I had no idea there was so much frustration out there."

Chiesel goes on the attack.

Chiesel's chin jutted out and he got within inches of Wally's face. Almost spitting as he spoke, he said, "I DON'T CARE what you think or what you were trying to do. You've got seventy-two hours to figure out how to fix this mess. Otherwise you are FIRED. And mark my words. I will personally make sure that you have no future in the meteorology industry or any other if I can help it! This is your problem, so figure it out." Chiesel stormed away.

Wally's normally jovial demeanor was reduced to a pathetic sack of sagging shoulders, a drooping head, and muffled whimpers. Wally knew he didn't have the luxury of self-pity, but at the moment he did not have any idea of where to start to try to make things right again. After some thought, he decided he should go speak with Jerome Numberman. Maybe Jerome would have some way of re-interpreting the survey results. Then the Media Center could blast out a press release highlighting some positive outcomes from the survey.

CHAPTER FOUR

A Call to the Summit

Wally found Jerome at his mahogany desk, busy crunching numbers. Jerome was mumbling under his breath, "These numbers are outrageous. There is no positive angle here."

Wally walked over to the edge of Jerome's desk. Jerome was going over the data from the surveys with a fine-tooth comb. Wally inquired, "Is there *any* redeeming story that can be found in these numbers that we can give to the Media Center?"

Jerome pushed his glasses down his nose and said, frowning with feigned patience, "No, Wally, thanks to the horrendous design of this survey I'm afraid there is nothing to be found in these results except mayhem."

Wally's momentary hope of finding a solution with Jerome was shattered, and he could feel his spirits sinking into despair. In a whiny voice he said, "All I wanted to do was make a difference."

Jerome took off his glasses and sighed. "I understand what you were trying to do, Wally, but one has to think several steps ahead in this organization. Ask before acting. Consider the possible outcomes. Sometimes doing nothing, at first, is better than doing something."

Wally looked at him quizzically. "But doing nothing doesn't accomplish anything."

"You'd be surprised," responded Jerome. "With age comes deliberation. Sometimes, actions taken in haste end up costing much more time to resolve down the road."

There was an awkward silence between the two. Wally, trying to deal with his fear, gazed into Jerome's eyes: "So, what do we do now?"

"I'm not sure," Jerome responded. "Whatever we do, it needs to be dramatic." Then he put his head down on his desk.

Wally slowly started shifting back and forth from

one foot to the other while puffing his chubby cheeks out on alternating sides. "Dramatic you say. Hmm...I think I have an idea."

"And what hare-brained scheme do you have in mind this time, Wally?" Jerome challenged.

For the first time in hours, Wally's face lit up. Stroking his chin, he exclaimed, "I think I know exactly what we need to do."

"Well, for crying out loud, don't just stand there with that goofy smile of yours. Tell me what you have in mind," Jerome said.

"We will call an emergency summit of all the clouds," Wally explained.

"What?" shrieked Jerome. "You plan to hold an emergency summit with clouds. And where pray tell do you plan to hold this summit of yours, at the top of Mount Everest?"

"I hadn't thought that far ahead yet, but the top of Mount Everest sounds like a splendid spot. I'll take that recommendation under advisement. I've been meaning to go see the Himalayas, and this is as good of a reason as any," said Wally, trying hard to sound authoritative again.

"You're going to have to pull that one off by yourself, kid. I am way too old to go to the top of Mount Everest, and it sounds like a recipe for disaster," Jerome grunted.

"Well, what are *you* going to do?" asked Wally.

Jerome rose from his desk and started scurrying around his office reaching for boxes in one of the closets. "I am going to start packing all of the things in my office so I am ready to leave when Chiesel Gordon fires both of us in less than seventy-two hours. He's holding me responsible for this debacle, and while you are off galli-vanting with the clouds on Mount Everest, I want to make sure I've collected all of my belongings. There's over thirty years of history in this office, if you haven't noticed, and I have no intention of leaving it here if I can help it."

"Why don't you take me seriously?" asked Wally.

"Wally, you are too young to be taken seriously, and to do so would be folly," Jerome answered.

"Just because I'm young doesn't mean I don't understand," argued Wally.

"You don't have perspective," countered Jerome.

"How can I gain perspective if you don't engage me in a discussion?" inquired Wally.

Jerome wrapped his hands around his head as if it was ready to explode. "Maybe we can talk while we are standing in the unemployment line. For now, GET OUT OF MY OFFICE. I want to enjoy my last few hours here in peace."

With that, Wally scurried out of Jerome's office. He did not have much time, and he had a lot to do.

Wally pulled out his cell phone and used it to send an instant message to one of his buddies, who worked as a communications specialist:

ALERT MEDIA: Emergency Summit Called by the Director of the Weather Customer Satisfaction Bureau. Tomorrow—9 A.M.—Mount Everest.

Next, Wally went outside and found a butterfly with brilliant wings of gold and turquoise. With his effusive charm Wally enlisted the butterfly's help, whispering all the details of his dilemma into its sympathetic ears. The butterfly fluttered its wings in acknowledgment and flitted off in search of more help. The butterfly told a bold hawk, who in turn told a stately eagle. The eagle soared to the top of a three-thousand-year-old redwood tree. The majestic redwood enlisted the help of a needle on its highest branch that was just a few days old. The fragile but brave needle scraped the edge of the sky and with a voice soft, yet more intense than all the brightest bells in the world, brought the news of Wally's emergency summit to the wind.

Once the wind got a whiff of the news, it screeched and howled across every square inch of the sky, grabbing the ears and imaginations of every cloud enveloping the planet. Wally was going to have a summit. What would come of it now would be up to him.

CHAPTER FIVE

Mama Chom

G asping for breath after a long, hard climb, Wally took his last step to reach the top of Mount Everest, with fifteen minutes to spare before the start of the emergency summit. He had just enough time to get his laptop and video projector set up. Given the arduous climb up the mountain, Wally hadn't been able to carry a screen with him, but he figured he could use one of the many dazzling snow peaks to project his computer presentation of the survey's results. As much as he hated to do it, the clouds needed to know the numbers. He was certain Jerome would have approved of his effective use of statistics. Surely the numbers from the survey results would motivate the clouds to find a solution. Wally knew that if he could get all the clouds to identify the root cause of customers' low satisfaction ratings, agree to a solution, and rally them to execute the solution, then he could save the WCSB's tarnished image and be a hero. All of this was very simple in theory, but Wally did not have a clue as to how it would play out. He had a presentation but he did not have a plan. There were too many variables that were out of his control.

"What an amazing place," thought Wally as he looked around. "I am standing over 29,000 feet in the sky on top of the world." The mountain's summit was like a throne in a kingdom of vast blue sky interrupted by endless rows of stark white peaks.

Out of nowhere Wally heard a soft and inviting voice: "Dear boy, who are you and why have you come to see me?"

Startled, Wally spun around in circles inquiring, "Who's speaking to me?"

"The Tibetan people call me Chomolungma, or 'mother goddess of the universe,'" responded the voice.

Wally meets "the mother goddess of the universe."

"But you can call me Mama Chom." Her sweet voice warmed the frigid air of the mountain, and Wally could feel himself relax as she spoke.

Mama Chom chuckled. "I am flattered by the title bestowed on me by the Tibetan people but, even being 60 million years old, I am a mere baby in the universe. It's true that I have witnessed quite a bit in my time. However, whatever little wisdom I have gained has been earned by learning to value both the past and the future. If you meld the insights derived from each, you can create a present, pregnant with possibilities."

Mama Chom studied the oval contours of Wally's face. She could see him weighing her words, but his dreamy blue eyes told her she was speaking in terms he did not understand. She decided she ought to save the philosophy lesson for later. She could tell he was going to need her help. She just wasn't sure what form it would take.

"What is your name, and why are you here?" asked Mama Chom.

"My name is Wally. You haven't heard the news? Didn't the wind tell you?"

"Tell me what, dear?"

Wally smiled and answered Mama Chom with pride. "I have called an emergency summit of all the clouds. I am the new Director of the Weather Customer Satisfaction Bureau. We conducted a survey and learned that people are very dissatisfied with the weather. I need to get to the bottom of it and develop an action plan to remedy the current situation. I am relying on the clouds to come up with some solutions. It's been nice speaking with you, Mama Chom, but the clouds will be arriving any moment now and I need to start this meeting on time. Thank you for accommodating us. The views are spectacular. Maybe you could arrange to have the heat turned up a bit."

Wally shuffled over to his laptop and started fiddling with his presentation. He was so preoccupied that he did not notice the huge swarm of clouds beginning to gather around the mountain's snowy peaks. The wind roared from the north, south, east, and west as it swept across the sky, pushing and pulling clouds into dense, white, billowy groups hovering in anticipation of the start of this momentous event. Never before had there been such a congregation of clouds.

CHAPTER SIX

Wait Five Minutes

Wally looked up from his computer and gasped in awe at what he saw. The clouds appeared to be self-organizing themselves into three distinct groups. One group was composed of large, puffy, dome-shaped, cotton-ball clouds. Although the clouds were in a group, they were detached and smug in their appearance. Wally marveled at the bright, bold, fresh curves of these youthful-looking giants. Thinking back on his studies, he knew that given their distinctive shapes these must be *cumulus* clouds.

The second group of clouds lacked the shapely character of the first group. These clouds were fused together in thick, gray layers. The flat, long string of clouds made members of the group indistinguishable from one another. By their appearance and demeanor,

Wally discerned that these clouds, classified by meteorologists as *stratus,* were older and more established than the first group of clouds.

The third group of clouds looked like they were trying to keep their distance from the cumulus and stratus groups of clouds. Wally observed that the clouds in this group were thin, wispy, and ready to dissipate. He reasoned that these had to be the oldest and most senior-ranking clouds present. Wally determined that these clouds were classified as *cirrus.*

Wally stepped back for a moment and tried to absorb the unearthly sight in front of him: cumulus clouds to his right, stratus clouds in the middle, and cirrus clouds to his left. A hush fell over the assembly. Wally cleared his throat and began.

"Good morning and welcome. My name is Wally, and on behalf of the Weather Customer Satisfaction Bureau I would like to thank you all for coming today. As you know, the WCSB has never held an emergency summit of clouds. We felt recent feedback from our customers around the world warranted such an event. Together, I believe we can find mutually beneficial solutions to our shared problem of people's attitudes and perceptions about the weather."

As Wally spoke there was whispering among the group of young cumulus clouds. "Did you hear that? This is the first emergency summit of all the clouds and we're here. Wow! Did you get a look at the group of stately cirrus clouds? Impressive. I think I recognize that cloud. Isn't he the famous?...."

Wally continued, "I thought we would start off this morning with a presentation of the results from a recent survey conducted by the WCSB to measure people's level of satisfaction with the weather." Wally flipped on the video projector and put up the first slide.

The elderly group of cirrus clouds started mumbling, "I told you this was going to be a waste of time. Why did we bother to come? There's nothing new under the sun, and now this kid is going to bore us with a didactic lecture on statistics. Kids these days think they can throw around fancy technology and call it communication. We've been around too long and know better."

The middle group, the stratus clouds, commented, "Let's reserve our judgment and see what Wally has to say."

Wally, oblivious to all the side conversations going on within the groups of clouds, launched into his spiel. "As you can see from this first graph, 91.9 percent of the respondents said they are very dissatisfied with the weather. Historical data from other sources suggest that this is not a new phenomenon. In fact, although there is not enough data to either confirm or deny it, our analysts have suggested that people were more upset with the weather fifty years ago than they are today. So that's some good news. We're improving aren't we?" Wally winked at the group of cumulus clouds. He felt it was important to win the support of the young clouds. He knew he was going to need some strong allies.

Wally continued, "Of course these results are understandable given the fact that today..."

The group of cirrus clouds started stirring, and some miffed clouds from the group could be heard saying, "Where is he getting this historical data? This guy's got some nerve. We have been working for years helping to produce stellar weather for people before this infantile bureaucrat was even in diapers."

The cumulus clouds looked bewildered by the older clouds' outbursts. "Why are the cirrus clouds so jaded?"

One of the clouds said, "We look up to them. I just don't understand why they're acting this way."

A particularly confrontational cloud yelled out to the group of cirrus clouds, "Why don't you guys just retire and let us take care of business!"

Thoroughly agitated, some of the cirrus clouds began to drift away.

The stratus clouds, which up to this point had been observing the whole scene and laughing at the antics,

The clouds are angry, and Wally is stumped.

did their best to act as a voice of reason. Over the growing crescendo of shouting back and forth between the cumulus and cirrus groups of clouds, one stratus cloud yelled, "Why don't we all calm down and see how we can work with each other to help Wally! That's why we're here, you know."

Wally's eyes looked like they were going to pop out of their sockets. In a matter of minutes, the emergency summit had turned into a cacophony of fighting voices. He had completely lost control of the situation. If he didn't do something quickly, all of the clouds would leave in an uproar.

CHAPTER SEVEN

Puff, Huff, and Stuff

Mama Chom had been watching this three-ring circus unfold and was quite distressed by the proceedings. Seeing Wally in dire trouble, she decided to intervene. Mama Chom cracked her knuckles and the faint, crisp chink of icicles could be heard. The sheet of hanging ice on which Wally had been projecting his presentation shattered into a million pieces on the ground. There was barely a break in the uproar of the clouds' infighting. Except for Wally, no one had heard Mama Chom.

Realizing she needed to do something more dramatic, Mama Chom lifted her arms above her head. At first, there was a low rumble followed by explosive booms and ballistic crashes, as snow and ice came smashing down the side of Mama Chom. At once the clouds stopped their bickering and a moment of deathly silence seized the summit's proceedings. In a powerful voice Mama Chom commanded, "STOP...STOP...STOP your self-serving, nonsensical arguing. You are not accomplishing anything!"

Then in a spellbinding voice, Mama Chom began, "There are so many different experiences and perspectives gathered here today. If you put your minds to it, and open your hearts and ears to one another, I know you will understand how to remedy this weather situation."

Wally blinked three times in rapid succession. Shaking off snow from his shoulders Wally said, "Mama Chom is right."

The clouds bellowed in unison, "Mama who?"

"Mama Chom," answered Wally. Seeing the clouds' confusion, Wally continued, "Mama Chom is short for Chomolungma, or Mount Everest. The Tibetan people regard her as 'mother goddess of the universe.'"

"What do we do now?" asked Puff, an earnest leader from the cumulus group of clouds.

Huff, one of the senior members of the cirrus group answered, "I think we should work in teams."

"That's a great idea," piped in Stuff, from the stratus group. "We should work in teams to figure out why people are so dissatisfied with the weather."

Wally clapped his hands together and exclaimed, "That's a splendid plan. Let's break everyone up into three groups. Puff, Huff, and Stuff, why don't you each form a group, but please make sure that it has a mix of cumulus, stratus, and cirrus clouds in it. As you work in your groups, please answer two questions. First, why do you think people are dissatisfied with the weather? Second, what solutions do you recommend to improve the current situation? After you have had a chance to work as teams we will reconvene and share insights and solutions"

Puff, Huff, and Stuff started gathering clouds around them and forming groups. The sky was a blur of clouds moving in every direction. Clouds of every size, shape, and age began intermingling with one another.

Wally watched the clouds rearrange themselves into diverse groups and looked very pleased. Things were definitely going in a positive direction. With a relieved grin, Wally sat down at his laptop to begin writing a report.

CHAPTER EIGHT

"Weather" You Like It or Not

Mama Chom leaned over and whispered into Wally's ear: "Your real work is just beginning. You don't have the luxury of sitting down right now—this is when the clouds will need your help the most. You need to circulate among the groups and listen to what they are saying. Try to learn something from all of the conversations. Even in these groups, there will likely be clashes of perspectives. It is your job to help each group benefit from its differences."

"I'm not sure if I know how to do what you are telling me. They didn't teach us that in meteorology school," responded Wally.

"I know, dear, but you will learn as you go along. I have full confidence in you," said Mama Chom as she gave Wally a gentle shove. "Now don't dilly-dally—get moving!"

Wally stood up and took inventory of the groups busy at work. They were deep in their conversations, and many of them were already writing lists of causes and solutions in the sky. Wally decided to mosey over to Puff's group. Puff was easy to like but maybe that was because Wally saw a lot of himself in the cloud. He was young, charismatic, and tireless in his energetic idealism. Wally stood behind Puff and almost got smacked across the face by one of Puff's wild gesticulations.

Puff was doing less facilitating and more pontificating. He had found a nice ridge on Mama Chom and was in full swing by the time Wally arrived. "People deserve better weather. We just don't do a good enough job of communicating."

One of the stratus clouds retorted, "What do you mean people deserve better?"

"Yeah, Puff," echoed a cirrus cloud. "You haven't been around long enough to know why things are the way they are. I can remember the great storms of the early twentieth century."

Three neophyte cumulus clouds chided in chorus, "The past doesn't matter."

"That's completely wrong," asserted one of the elderly cirrus clouds. "You can't fix the present if you don't have an appreciation and knowledge of the past."

"Look," Puff continued, "we need to fix this problem by going forward. People around the world are being devastated by horrendous storms. Lives are being turned upside down."

One of the stratus clouds interrupted Puff. "Devastating storms represent only a fraction of the problem," he said condescendingly. "Besides, we can't control storms—we never have and we never will."

"Wait a minute. Maybe Puff is right," asserted another cirrus cloud. "As older clouds we tend to be so focused on how things have been that we do not spend enough time imagining how things can be different."

Wally interjected, "People are not dissatisfied because of a few natural disasters. Those are freaks of nature, and that's not what's driving down our customer satisfaction numbers."

"Okay," fumed another cloud, "then what is?"

"I am convinced," Puff said, as he pounded his fist in the air, "that people's general discontent with the weather is more a function of the unpredictable nature of the weather. What if we could find a way to keep people better informed of what to expect? Then the weather would not be such a surprise to them. Won't that equate to better satisfaction ratings?"

"Yeah, but how do you propose we do that?" asked one of the stratus clouds. A silence fell upon the group. Wally could see all of the clouds deep in thought. He took this opportunity to leave the group and walk toward another one.

Wally next visited Huff's group. Without a doubt, Huff was the most famous cloud in attendance at the summit. He had lived through more seasons and visited more continents than any other cloud in recorded history. Despite his feathery, stretched, frail appearance, Huff was a *tour de force*. Many of the young cumulus clouds idolized him. They were all sitting in front of him, as he waxed lyrically about the challenges of satisfying customers.

Huff is a hero to the young clouds

"You see," Huff explained, "customers have been misled for years by quack meteorologists. These two-bit weather-know-it-alls rely on poor instrumentation instead of the age-old wisdoms and instincts handed down by Mother Nature to animals. Have you ever known an animal to complain about the weather? Of course not! They adapt. They anticipate. Humans, I'm afraid, have been roped into believing what they hear on TV during a two-minute weather exposé that amounts to little more than glorified guesswork. Except for mariners sailing the sea, farmers toiling the earth, and outdoor enthusiasts communing with nature, how many people have you seen go outside and look at the clouds, smell the air, observe the moon, and take note of the winds' ever-changing direction?

"Herein lies our problem. I, for one, miss the kind of connection we had with people in the past. People used to lie in fields on their backs and look up at us, crafting grand visions of our contours in their wild imaginations and reading great meaning from our movements. They simply do not connect with us viscerally anymore. They've distanced themselves from nature in this fundamental way."

All the cumulus, stratus, and cirrus clouds were nodding in agreement at Huff's pearls of wisdom. Wally, on the other hand, was disturbed by what he was hearing. He could not let Huff brainwash them. Meteorologists like him had been instrumental in improving peoples' lives by providing timely information. Even though the information was not always up-to-date or accurate, it was more than people had before all the advances in technology. Wally really had to take issue with Huff's comments and did not feel all of the clouds, particularly the young cumulus ones, should be persuaded by such a lopsided view.

But before Wally even had a chance to speak, he realized Huff was pointing at him and continuing his pontificating. "Our dear friend Wally here is a prime example of what I'm talking about. Although none of us would question his well-intentioned efforts to make a difference and improve the current state of affairs, he is a victim of the system. He, like so many others, is just a poor unassuming slave to the paradigm they're stuck in. We can liberate him today and everyone else in the world for that matter from their unnecessary suffering. The solution is simple: Stop trying to predict the weather and learn how to accept its natural ebbs and flows."

Wally was opening his mouth to defend his profession and perspective when he felt Mama Chom tug on his pant leg.

"Wally," Mama Chom implored quietly, "resist the urge to speak. Try to put your ego aside. What do you notice going on in Huff's group?"

"I hear a lot of nonsense, that's what I hear," responded Wally. "I have a responsibility as leader of this summit to set the record straight."

"Think again, dear," coached Mama Chom. "Earlier this morning the young cumulus clouds and the older cirrus clouds were at each other's throats. Neither group was open to the other's perspective. Although Huff is engaged in more of a one-way conversation, the cumulus clouds are gaining a valuable insight into the attitudes, beliefs, and values of a different generation through his stories. That is the beginning of getting these generations to work together. Now you must find a way to seize the group's openness to each other and help them move toward identifying solutions that can emerge from their new understanding. It's an evolving process. Don't be capsized by the irregularity of the moment; be attuned to the possibilities that rise from the process."

Wally's face was wrinkled with knots of confusion. "You sure speak funny, Mama Chom. I'm not sure if I understood everything you just told me, but I think the bottom line is that I should keep my mouth shut and move on to the last group and the rest will take care of itself."

"That's more or less what I said, Wally. You are a fast learner," chuckled Mama Chom.

Wally walked toward the last group, wondering what was in store for him there. He hoped he would not have to swallow any more of his ego. He wasn't sure if there was room in his stomach after withstanding Huff's diatribes.

Stuff was a huge, long, flat, gray cloud with a steady monotone voice. Stuff's drab disposition did not seem to dampen the energy of the group. An adolescent cumulus cloud was busy scribbling notes in the sky under the watchful eye of an experienced cirrus cloud that corrected him as he recorded the group's discussion.

Stuff addressed the group: "I propose we turn our attention to analyzing the evolving role of the meteorologist. By doing so I believe we may gain some valuable insights into people's dissatisfaction with the weather and move toward some positive solutions. Let's start by taking a poll. How many of you feel people's perceptions of the weather have been hampered or improved by the work of meteorologists?"

There was a brief pause as Stuff and his helpers tallied the results, and then he continued: "Okay, by the show of hands we have an almost perfect split between everyone's opinions. Why don't we explore each opinion in greater detail?"

A cantankerous cirrus cloud jumped in and said, "Meteorologists are slaves to technology."

The adolescent cumulus cloud acting as the group's record keeper countered, "But technology is just a tool." The cirrus cloud standing next to him reprimanded him for interfering with the conversation and forgetting his role as a record keeper.

"I feel technology has become too invasive," asserted another cirrus cloud.

"I think he's right. Technology can't be the solution but maybe it can play some sort of role," said a stratus cloud.

"I, for one, have seen a noticeable difference in people's expectations," observed another stratus cloud. "People plan their lives around the information they receive. Technology is misleading meteorologists and people alike. Meteorologists don't use it properly and people are poor consumers of information."

An impatient cirrus cloud challenged, "Is this about educating people or managing people's expectations? I'm not interested in being in the education business. I have enough to do coordinating all my activities with the sun, moon, stars, and the seas. Throwing meteorologists and customers into the mix is not in my job description."

Stuff responded, "I can appreciate how you feel, and I'm quite certain you are not alone in your feelings. What I'm hearing, though, is that figuring out a way to manage customer's expectations should play a central part in whatever solution we devise."

CHAPTER NINE

The Dawn of the World Wide Weather Network

Wally checked his watch. He could not believe how much time had passed. The sun was already beginning to set. He better reconvene all the groups. Wally had been reflecting on Mama Chom's advice. Somehow he had to take the diverse perspectives of all the clouds and mold a workable solution.

Wally shouted above all of the conversations, "Will everyone please regroup?"

The clouds stopped what they were doing and, to Wally's surprise, stayed put in their mixed groups rather than return to their original ones of cumulus, stratus, and cirrus clouds.

"I think the best way to proceed is to ask Puff, Huff, and Stuff to report on their group's findings. Puff, would you kick it off?" said Wally.

Puff floated gracefully to the front, where Wally was standing. After rearranging some of his bulbous features, Puff began: "Our group wrestled with trying to reconcile the past and the future. Some members of the group felt it was important to understand the past, while many of us, myself included, felt that being overly fixated on the past would not help us understand how to fix things going forward. Thinking about it now, it's probably a little bit of both. As far as coming up with solutions, we're not sure of the exact nature of one, but we concluded that if we want to improve people's satisfaction with the weather we need to find a way to keep people better informed." Puff rejoined his group, where cumulus, stratus, and cirrus clouds greeted him with high fives.

Wally grinned. He couldn't believe that these were the same clouds that were ready to get into a brawl earlier in the day. "Thanks, Puff. Your group has given us some good things to think about. Does anyone have any reactions to what Puff shared with us?"

Wally hears good news at last.

One of the youngest cumulus clouds in the assembly piped up, "I appreciate Puff's focus on the future, and his determination to uncover new ways of thinking and doing things. I have a unique perspective. Despite my age, the most influential forces in my life have been clouds with a rich knowledge of the past. I consider myself aggressive and forward thinking, but it stems from a keen appreciation and curiosity about the past. The past is my template. I benchmark everything against it. I seek knowledge of the past."

Another young cumulus cloud began: "That's right. I really relate to what my peer is saying. I feel that sometimes others assume that my opinions and values have been formed in a void, when in fact I have taken the time and care to understand the history and background of a situation before acting or speaking."

Mama Chom nudged Wally and coached him to acknowledge the comments being made. "What I'm hearing is that valuing the past and the future has nothing to do with age," said Wally. "I think that's an important point. Let's move on to the next group."

Turning to Huff, Wally did his best to conceal his frustration. "Your group had some interesting ideas. Would you share your findings with us?"

Huff's frail but commanding presence caused a hush to fall across the assembly. "Before beginning, I would like to say that I found this process thoroughly enjoyable. I almost never get a chance to meet with my colleagues anymore and I realized today there are so many interesting clouds out there. It was an honor and a privilege to share my stories and opinions with the group, especially with some of the fresh clouds in the sky. They indulged me, and, dare I say, they perhaps even learned a thing or two."

One of the cumulus clouds from Huff's group cheered, "You're awesome, Huff!"

Huff continued, "While I recognize that I may have been heavy-handed in my judgmental remarks about meteorologists and customers, our group gained some important insights about today's dissatisfied customers by analyzing the past. Prior to the technology that is prominent today, people were easier to please because they were more accepting of the weather's natural ups and downs. Some say ignorance is bliss, and while I don't agree with the cliché entirely, I think there is some truth to it. And ignorance is more akin to our natural state of being. Even as clouds, our knowledge of future weather patterns is far from perfect or complete. So our group concluded that we need to find additional ways, besides technology, to get people to be more open to the unpredictable patterns of the weather."

When Huff finished his remarks, the whole assembly, including Wally, gave Huff a standing ovation. Huff blushed from all the attention being showered on him and bowed his head in humble acknowledgment.

Wally shivered with glee. Whatever remnants of resentment he had felt toward Huff melted away.

Although he did not fully agree with Huff, he felt like he had a new perspective—one that combined his zeal for the cutting-edge technical developments in meteorology with an appreciation of the past. When the applause died down, Wally asked the members of the assembly to share their reactions.

A stratus cloud began: "Huff has touched my imagination and reminded me what it means to be a cloud. It's easy to forget the nature of our relationship with people, each other, and the technocrats who try to measure, and discern the meaning of our movements."

One dreamy cloud mused, "Maybe we have a cosmic role to play in all of this. Perhaps humanity is heading down a destructive path in its earnest efforts to make life more stable and predictable. In essence, life is chaotic. Knowing the weather appears trivial but has much grander implications. It's a natural but dangerous desire for control that neither exists nor is in anyone's best interests to pursue. I believe it's our responsibility to enlighten people."

A rowdy cloud yelled out, "Hey, save the philosophy for a book." Scanning the assembly, Wally sensed it was time to move on, and so he invited Stuff to address the group.

By this point, everyone was engaged by the summit's proceedings and anxious to hear what Stuff and his group had discussed. Stuff made a wide sweeping gesture with his hands and addressed the assembly: "Consider the following question: Have meteorologists made a positive or negative impact on people's level of satisfaction with the weather?" Stuff paused for a moment to give the clouds an opportunity to reflect on his question and then continued.

"Our group was split in its opinion. Some members felt that both meteorologists and people have become too dependent upon technology. People plan their lives around the information provided to them by meteorologists who use imprecise tools. Other clouds in our group felt that technology could be used to do a better job of managing people's expectations of the weather. Given the results of the survey Wally shared with us earlier, today's technology seems incapable of living up to this promise. Technology is here to stay, but for the foreseeable future the rate of its improvement will not match people's current high expectations. So where does that leave us? As one astute member of our group pointed out, we are not in the business of educating our customers on the intricate arts of predicting the weather. These secrets have been passed down to us generation after generation and cannot be shared with humans. We don't have the language or the means to do so even if we wanted to. We concluded that any workable solution must figure out how to use meteorologists and technology to manage people's expectations."

"Thank you, Stuff," said Wally, who seemed a bit dazed by Stuff's soliloquy.

"Where do we go from here?" asked a cloud.

Wally wiggled his nose a few times before responding. For a moment it looked like he might be speechless until Mama Chom whispered into his ear, "Wally, recap the findings of the groups and help them synthesize the findings into solutions."

Wally flipped on his video projector and aimed it at a new wall of ice and started typing a list on his laptop. "We have an excellent collection of thoughts from all the groups. Now we need to devise a solution. Let's start by summarizing the findings of each group. Puff, your group believes we need to keep people better informed. Huff's group reminded us that we should help people to become more accepting of the weather and its unpredictable nature. Stuff's group concluded we can manage people's expectations of the weather with the aid of meteorologists and technology."

Wally consulted with Mama Chom, muttering under his breath, "What do I do now?"

"Ask them to look for the interrelationships among the three summaries. This will naturally lead you to some solutions," Mama Chom instructed.

Wally questioned the assembly, "What's the interrelationship among all of these ideas?" Clouds started raising their hands to speak and Wally called on them as fast as he could.

"Well, if people were better informed of what can be predicted and what cannot be predicted about the weather, they would become more accepting of its uncertainties."

"Good," Wally encouraged. "What else?"

"If meteorologists had access to more information, they could improve the accuracy of their reports."

"Okay," Wally said, as he nodded.

"What if meteorologists could know the gap between what they can forecast and what is subject to change?" said another cloud, thinking out loud.

"Do you mean the changes in weather that not even we know?" another cloud asked.

"Yes, I mean the changes that neither we, nor any of the other crucial components of the weather—such as the wind, sun, moon, stars, and seas—can know in advance," responded the first cloud.

Wally raised a finger above his head. "That strikes

"Yes!"

me as an excellent way of managing people's expectations. What do the rest of you think? Will that work?"

In almost perfect unison the assembly of clouds said, "Yes!"

"But how do we help meteorologists assess the gap between what they can forecast and what they cannot?" bellowed several clouds.

"What if we set up a network?" offered one of the youngest cumulus clouds.

"A what?" shrieked a cirrus cloud.

Wally jumped in with an explanation. "What I think he meant was the establishment of a communications network. Is that right?"

"Yes," answered the young cumulus cloud.

"And what good would that do? Meteorologists already have barometers, temperature gauges, and a host of other instruments. What is this communications network going to do differently?" challenged another cirrus cloud.

"I see where he is going," said a stratus cloud. "All of

us could use the network to share information. Then if there was a way to collect the information centrally, it could be disseminated to meteorologists all over the world."

"Yeah... That's a fantastic idea. We could call it the World Wide Weather network, or WWW for short," said another stratus cloud.

"We'd all have to agree to cooperate with one another and be willing to work, and listen to each other, the way we have been doing at this summit, if this plan is going to work," said another cumulus cloud.

"All right, so if we enlist the help of the wind and precipitation to transport the information among us, then all we would need is a way of centrally collecting and disseminating the information to meteorologists," explained Huff. "Wally, can you and your crew at the WCSB set up a mechanism for doing this?"

Wally hadn't been this excited since he had been named director of the WCSB. He was jumping up and down and practically screamed, "YES...YES!!"

There was a tremendous roar of cheers as the clouds began patting each other on the back. Regaining his composure, Wally tried to bring the emergency summit to some sort of official close, but it was too late. Cirrus and cumulus clouds were already floating off together at breakneck speed, yakking away. Even the clouds wishing to linger and speak with Wally were whisked away by the wind's exuberant movements. Within a minute Wally was standing alone on Mount Everest. He began packing up his equipment.

"Wally," Mama Chom called, "what did you learn today?"

"It's amazing what can be accomplished when we listen to each other and learn to respect and appreciate values different from our own. I guess we all have different experiences. I can't thank you enough, Mama

Chom. This summit was going to be a fiasco, but you helped me create an effective environment where a variety of generations of clouds felt safe and comfortable sharing their feelings and thoughts. They did all the work. I really didn't even do anything. You know," Wally chuckled, "if this is what leadership is all about I am well suited for it. Chiesel Gordon even said that 'laziness' was one of my outstanding attributes. Thanks for everything."

"My pleasure, Wally," answered Mama Chom. "Do you have a plan for how you will implement the clouds' solution when you go back to the WCSB?"

"Not exactly," answered Wally.

"Why don't you work with Jerome Numberman to set up the central repository for collecting and disseminating the information from the clouds?" suggested Mama Chom.

"But he doesn't know anything about computers!" retorted Wally.

"And you don't know anything about the WCSB,"

countered Mama Chom. "Maybe if you work together, you will be able to implement a solution sooner rather than later and save both of your jobs in the process."

"You've got a good point there," said Wally, starting to scamper down the trail leading off the mountain. "I better get moving."

Mama Chom watched Wally to make sure he was safe. Then with a long sigh she cast her eyes into the vast sky above her. It was filled with lingering hues of brilliant orange and red as the sun set, and not a cloud could be seen for miles. The moon was glowing and the stars were already beginning to twinkle. Mama Chom smiled to herself. She was going to sleep well tonight.

CHAPTER TEN

On Cloud Nine

After climbing down Mount Everest, Wally spent the rest of his trip writing a report of the summit's proceedings for Jerome. He wanted to make sure Jerome was fully briefed before he spoke to him. On his way home, Wally stopped at the WCSB office and slipped his report under Jerome's door. He knew Jerome liked to come in before anyone else and read the newspaper. Wally wanted to be there when Jerome arrived.

Wally was up at the crack of dawn, but he was confident his adrenaline would pull him through. The next couple of hours would determine whether he had a job or not. Equally important was his commitment to the clouds to set up the World Wide Weather network (WWW). Wally did not want to let them down.

Wally burst into Jerome's office. Except for pieces of the WCSB computer system that had been in the corner of the office three days ago and the mahogany desk, the room was completely empty. Jerome was sitting at his desk reading Wally's report. And by the look on his face, Wally was afraid Jerome's mouth had become unhinged. As soon as Jerome saw Wally enter, he ran over to the computer and began picking up the pieces.

"Don't just stand there, son," he said, turning to Wally. "Roll up your sleeves and give me a hand with this blasted computer. We've got some serious work to do. You need to show me how to use this contraption if we are going to get this WWW network working before Chiesel Gordon gives us the boot."

"Gentlemen, gentlemen," a familiar booming voice said.

Jerome and Wally poked their heads outside the door and saw Chiesel Gordon barreling down the hall.

"You are heroes! It's over all the news wires":

CLOUDS AND THE WCSB WORK TOGETHER TO
BUILD A NEW FUTURE FOR METEOROLOGISTS
AND CUSTOMERS.

"This is fantastic!" said Chiesel as he almost knocked Wally over with his pat on the back. "This is tremendous—clouds are collaborating with the WCSB and its meteorologists to improve the quality of weather information. Have you two got this WWW network up and running yet? Our technology department informed me five minutes ago that reams and reams of data are already pouring in from clouds all over the world. Can you guys get that WWW thing working by lunch? I want to make sure the Media Center maximizes the punch of this story. This is a historic moment. Wally, if you keep up this kind of work you will take my place at the helm of this great organization in no time at all. Don't get any ideas—it will be after I retire, of course. Jerome, keep showing Wally the ropes. Your tutelage has transformed this kid from chump to champ. Now don't let me hold you gentlemen up any further. There's work to be done."

Wally and Jerome heard Chiesel Gordon exclaiming, "Bravo...Bravo...Bravo," as he went down the hallway.

Wally and Jerome looked each other in the eyes with huge smiles plastered over their faces. They were definitely on Cloud Nine.

Part II

From Fable into Practice

CHAPTER ELEVEN

What We Can Learn
from the Story

HOW DO YOU RELATE to those of different ages within your workplace? Do older individuals irritate you with their traditional ways? Perhaps younger colleagues have you wondering what has happened to the work ethic. Disagreements between the ages have existed throughout history. In fact, people have always asked, "What's wrong with that younger generation?" Wally, Jerome, Chiesel, and the clouds all faced the same kind of challenges in our story.

Younger individuals need to understand the experiences driving the values, assumptions, decisions, and behaviors of older workers. This does not mean that they need to accept all of them. But the disdain that they sometimes display for the "old-timers" mistakenly discounts the wisdom many of these individuals possess. Just because a decision *can* be made quickly, for instance, doesn't mean that it *needs* to be made quickly. Sometimes actions taken in haste end up costing much more time down the road.

At the same time, many older individuals need to find a better balance between using the past as a reference and finding a means for embracing the future. Often, a younger employee's ideas are dismissed, simply because of his or her lack of experience. Mature workers are sometimes put off by the exuberance of youth, choosing to "hide" behind their veteran status, rather than taking a minute to listen and make a reasoned decision. To maintain a productive working environment, workers of all ages need to develop an appreciation for each other's perspective on the past, present, and future.

The introduction of electronic technology over the past twenty years has also produced a fundamental split between younger and older generations. Older generations are apt to look to this technology as a solution in itself, while younger generations see it as a tool to help find a solution. This can become divisive when older individuals, frustrated by the challenges of technology, resent the time it takes to learn the new tools before actually using them to do something useful. Younger workers look at learning this technology as an investment in learning and personal marketability not just for that job but also for future jobs and opportunities.

As we saw in the fable, Jerome Numberman essentially discarded the technology placed before him in favor of that with which he was familiar. Alternately, Wally was using technology to survey customers without the proper regard for its impact. These types of situations are played out daily in businesses throughout the United States. Regardless of their age, workers need to appreciate the benefits and the liabilities of using technology. How every generation perceives these benefits and liabilities depends a great deal upon its experiences in youth.

KEY POINTS TO REMEMBER

■ Wally threw himself into his new job with enthusiasm, but he made the mistake of acting without consulting others. Veteran managers have discovered that there is more to most major decisions than meets the eye. If you're new to a position, it's always best to seek out others who have been around for a while to gather their insights. While each may give you a different perspective, comparing these perspectives will help you understand the potential opportunities and pitfalls.

■ Wally made the assumption that because his predecessors had failed in conducting a customer survey, their techniques were out-of-date or "old school." But by limiting his perspective to this one reference point, he made a nearly fatal error. It can be easy to judge the methods of those in the past without regard to the technology and reasoning with which they had to deal. Doing so, however, can result in dismissing valuable information prematurely. It's always helpful to ask about the previous methodology before dismissing it as irrelevant.

■ Jerome Numberman seemed to have drawn a conclusion about Wally's survey efforts before hearing him out. It is sometimes too easy to leap to judgment about a particular issue simply because you've worked in the organization for a long time. But it is important to reserve your criticism until you have a chance to ask the right questions. Rather than simply dismissing Wally's idea out of hand, Jerome could have been more helpful by asking questions and attempting to shape Wally's efforts.

■ Jerome also made the assumption that Wally and all of his generation think alike. In doing so, he was probably painting Wally with the same broad brush of inexperience as other bright young talent. While we can observe the patterns in the behaviors of a generation, we must also be careful not to overgeneralize. It is important to ask questions and qualify our assumptions before taking action.

■ Wally's youthful exuberance was both a blessing and a curse. On one hand, his enthusiasm produced the energy and focus to embark on a bold idea. On the other, it blinded him to the obvious hurdles that almost proved insurmountable. When embarking on a new venture it is critical to maintain the perspective necessary to prepare for the inevitable challenges ahead. Had Wally been able to temper his exuberance, he would have taken a more measured approach to the project.

■ Young people can be impatient to ascend to a position of authority too quickly. Unfortunately, this may place them in situations beyond their present capabilities. One has to wonder about the choices Wally might have made had he more experience before being placed in this situation. While it can be frustrating to wait your turn, sometimes that's the best thing that can happen.

■ It is important to remember the impact of the written word. Wally's memorandum to the board of directors was decisive, but ill-timed. In his enthusiasm to begin, he demonstrated his lack of perspective about the situation. This, in turn, created some concern within the organization's leadership about his fitness for the position. Experience teaches one to exercise care before sending correspondence with wide-ranging impact.

■ While young workers' exuberance can sometimes get the better of them, veteran managers must supervise these young people using moderation. Chiesel Gordon was justifiably angry about Wally's initiation of the survey. But berating him loudly so others could hear without first gathering the facts was inappropriate as well. Calling Wally's survey "a reckless act of madness" is a sure way to alienate Wally and many within the organization. A short, but devastating exchange like this will dash the hopes of any worker regardless of age.

■ One of the biggest challenges young workers face is being taken seriously by veteran colleagues. Wally faced this obstacle with Jerome Numberman. The keys to succeeding in this environment are to be patient and well prepared. Successful young workers develop an ability to put themselves in the mind of the older colleague. This enables them to develop an empathy for that person's concerns. They also prepare carefully to make sure their suggestions and arguments are persuasive. Finally, they recognize the value of patience and choose the right time to make their suggestions.

■ One of the things that Wally discovers in his trek to Mount Everest is the opportunity for reflection. Taking time to consider options, brainstorm ideas, or simply recharge your batteries can be one of the most rewarding things you can do for yourself. While difficult to accomplish in many hectic workplaces, successful young workers learn over time that getting away to think helps clear the head to focus on the larger issues.

■ On the mountains with Mama Chom, Wally discovers the value of mentoring and age-old wisdom. As in Wally's case, this discovery sometimes has to come when your back is against the wall. It can be difficult for young people to accept the suggestions of veteran workers. But those who accept them generally find they can be more valuable than any kind of classroom learning.

■ By observing the clouds in action, Wally discovered how impressionable they can be. Some of the younger cumulus clouds practically worshipped certain older cirrus clouds. Yet some of these older clouds expressed disdain for any ideas of change within the system. That, in turn, bewildered the younger clouds. Wally began to understand how much of a role perception can play in guiding the behavior of different ages.

■ As the summit evolved, Wally watched with fascination as the disparate groups began to work in concert. Sometimes, listening and quietly facilitating can be the most effective means for developing relationships among different groups. The more these groups began to mingle, the more they found they had in common.

■ Toward the end of the summit, one of the older cirrus clouds observes that older clouds tend to be so focused on how things have been that they do not spend enough time imagining how things can be different. Anyone, regardless of age, can get comfortable or even stuck in a rut. But the older one gets, the more chance there is that this will happen. It is critical to periodically revisit systems and practices to evaluate their effectiveness.

■ As Huff accuses Wally of being a "victim of the system," Wally is tempted to respond in defense. But Mama Chom cautions him to resist the urge and put his ego aside. Sometimes it's better to swallow one's pride. If the criticism is unfair, chances are that will be revealed over time. Wally has to remember that he is the leader and that everyone is watching his actions and hanging on his words.

■ As Chiesel Gordon bursts into Jerome's office upon Wally's return, Wally discovers how fickle the line can be between success and failure. That lesson will serve him well for the rest of his working life.

CHAPTER TWELVE

Questions for Thought
and Discussion

THESE QUESTIONS WILL HELP YOU analyze what the characters in the fable did or failed to do; what better alternatives they had; and how they can be more effective in the future.

■ Why would Jerome Numberman be so skeptical of the survey Wally had developed? How might he have modified his approach to remain honest but more encouraging with Wally?

■ What steps might Wally have taken prior to sending Jerome the results of his survey so as to build a better relationship with this workplace veteran?

■ How might Chiesel Gordon have better handled the survey situation with Wally after discovering the initial results?

■ During the summit on Mount Everest, Wally watches as the older cirrus clouds express their jaded views about weather forecasting before the entire group. What strategies might he use the next time this type of thing begins to happen?

■ The younger cumulus clouds appeared to be exuberant at the beginning of the summit, only to become disillusioned by the comments of the older cirrus clouds. How might Wally deal with this in the future as new clouds appear on the horizon?

■ At the beginning of the summit, Wally addresses the group with a presentation filled with the history of weather forecasting. This is met with disdain by many, who shout out comments and objections. How might Wally improve his approach when making presentations to large gatherings?

■ During the summit, the middle-aged stratus clouds attempt to be the peacemakers. How might Wally have better used this to his advantage in persuading the entire group?

■ During the summit, Mama Chom counsels the young Wally to seize the opportunities to lead as they appear. What strategies should he have put into place to help him do a better job of anticipating opportunities?

■ Throughout the summit, Mama Chom attempts to mentor Wally as he leads this unwieldy gathering. How might Wally have better taken advantage of her counsel and wisdom?

■ Through a twist of fate, Wally has gone from heel to hero due to this survey and summit? What steps should he now take to make the most of this momentum?

CHAPTER THIRTEEN

A Quiz for the Reader

THIS BRIEF SELF-TEST focuses on your own attitudes and behaviors. It will help you develop strategies for working and managing successfully in a multigenerational workplace.

■ Which of your assumptions about coworkers older or younger than you later turned out to be false?

■ What is your first emotion when someone younger challenges your experience or expertise? What tends to be your immediate reaction?

■ In the fable, Wally learned that different age groups will learn to work together provided the right environment exists to do so. How might you create that environment within your workplace if it doesn't already exist?

■ If you were supervising a group of people ranging in age from 18 to 60, how would you go about integrating the differences in their attitudes and experiences?

■ Many times, conflicts between younger and older workers come down to an interpretation of work ethic. As a manager, how would you work to resolve these differences and promote an appreciation for each other's point of view?

■ The members of Generation X and the Millennials will have a significant impact on the way work is accomplished in most organizations over time. How do you predict this will change in your present work environment?

■ Gen Xers tend to be skeptical of the objectives of most employers. As a supervisor, what steps would you take to overcome this skepticism?

■ The members of Generation X tend to be focused on outcome, while the Millennials require more direct supervision. If you were supervising both groups in the same work environment, what strategies would you use to manage each effectively?

■ Many Millennials have come of age learning how to "work the system" by watching the behavior of parents, teachers, politicians, and others they see in the media. What steps can you take, as a supervisor, to prevent these young people from applying those strategies within your work environment?

■ Consider the different generations within your present work environment. What steps can you take today to build better relations with those around you?

CHAPTER FOURTEEN

Frequently Asked Questions and Answers About Generational Differences

WHY DOES the multigenerational workforce present so many issues, particularly for managers? What are the most common questions raised? Before we list the questions—and provide some answers—here is a thumbnail description of the four generations in today's workforce and the "labels" most often attached to them.

There are presently some 300 million people living in the United States. They can be divided into four generations. The oldest of these groups we chose to call Matures. This is a term originally coined by Walker Smith and Ann Clurman for their 1997 book, *Rocking the Ages*. Matures are defined as having been born prior to 1946 and currently comprise some 63 million people within the U.S. population. Some writers have divided the older and younger halves of this generation into Veterans (or G.I.s) and Silents, respectively.

The Matures gave birth to the so-called Baby Boom generation. This group is defined as having been born from 1946 through 1964. The term "baby boom" was coined by Landon Jones for his 1980 book, *Great Expectations*. In this book, Jones chronicles the impact that "Boomers" are having as they age through society.

Because of their generation's size (some 77 million strong), Boomers have a significant influence on every aspect of society.

Baby Boomers are unique in the sense that they have given birth to one and a half generations. The older of these two groups is the so-called Generation X. "Xers" are defined as having been born from 1965 through 1980. There are conflicting opinions on the origin of the term. Some attribute it to the so-called Beat movement of the 1950s. Others attribute it to a novel written by Canadian Douglas Copeland and published in 1990, which he titled *Generation X*. In any event, the American media adopted the term at the beginning of the 1990s and has used it to identify this generation ever since. The U.S. Bureau of the Census estimates Generation X to be some 50 million strong.

Because the Baby Boomers produced two waves of children, the youngest generation in the workforce is a product of both younger Boomers and the older half of Generation X. Terms associated with them include Generation Y, Generation WHY, Net-Geners, Nexters, and Echo Boomers to name a few. Over time, the term "Millennials" has become the preferred moniker. This term was originally coined by William Strauss and Neil Howe, who have written extensively on the impact of generational differences. The Millennials were born from 1981 through 1999. They are currently some 81 million strong.

FREQUENTLY ASKED QUESTIONS

As we study the generations within American society, managers continue to express a number of common concerns about their differences. Here are some answers to a variety of questions we hear frequently:

Work Ethic

■ *Different generations seem to subscribe to different beliefs about what it means to work hard or contribute to the organization. How do you define those differences?*

These differences depend, to a large degree, on what each generation was taught as children. The Matures, for instance, grew up in the midst of war-time shortages and economic depression. They have always worked hard and paid their dues.

Even in better times, they have continued these ways simply because this is the ethic with which they feel most comfortable.

Baby Boomers came of age in the midst of tremendous economic expansion, learning to use all the convenience-oriented products that came on the market during their youth. Because of the size of their generation, they were also the focus of everyone's attention. Boomers have always put in long hours because of how closely they associate their occupation with their identity. Even as they edge into retirement, we predict that most of them will still live to work.

Having watched their parents, the Baby Boomers, put in these long hours, Generation Xers have developed a different perspective on work. They do not necessarily equate productive work with long hours. Instead, they look for ways to work smarter, resulting in fewer hours but greater output. This is the reason why Boomers and Matures sometimes accuse those in Generation X of "punching the clock."

The Millennials are coming of age in an era of technology and rapid change. Many of them honestly wonder why machines don't do many of the mundane tasks they are asked to perform in entry-level positions. They have been heavily influenced to believe that every job should match the same level of stimulation they receive from a video game. As this generation matures into the workforce, some of these perceptions will change. But this group will also alter society's interpretation of work ethic as they go.

Work/Life Balance

■ *What are the generations' differences in beliefs about work and the rest of their lives?*

Matures and Baby Boomers have often devoted themselves to their work at the expense of family life and personal growth. This has been felt most severely by their children, the Xers. As a result, Xers have developed a focus on a clear balance between work and the other aspects of their lives.

With the oldest of the Millennials now in their mid-twenties, it is difficult to predict their attitudes toward work/life balance. But one might suspect that they will place the same emphasis on this issue as their older brethren, the Xers.

Career Development

■ *Each generation has taken its own approach to career development. How do these approaches differ?*

Career development, as it is interpreted today, was not part of the equation for many Matures. As young adults, they were conditioned to believe that one should be thankful to have a job. The ultimate goal was to move up within an organization, even if it meant working grueling hours. The one thing no one wanted to do was leave the organization.

Career development, as a genre, emerged with the Baby Boomers. The landmark book by Richard Bolles, *What Color Is Your Parachute?,* heralded the beginning of the Boomers' proactive focus on job-related self-determination. While this awareness opened new doors for them, especially after mass layoffs began in the 1980s, relatively few rushed for the exits. Instead, they have traditionally focused on taking the initiative to manage their careers within one organization or at least one industry.

As the members of Generation X began to enter the workplace in the 1980s, they took a proactive approach to career development from the get-go. Having witnessed the mergers, acquisitions, and layoffs their elders suffered, they resolved early on to take charge of their own destiny. The key word for them is *versatility*. The more degrees or experiences they can acquire, the more they feel they are able to manage opportunity. While some accuse them of having no loyalty to an organization, to them loyalty to one's self is paramount.

Millennials will enter the full-time workforce in large numbers over the next decade. But there is little doubt that they will place the same emphasis on versatility as Generation X. They have come of age with a media that lionizes executives who have rocketed to the top and parents who place extraordinary emphasis on getting the best education and positioning for future success. At the same time, the size of their generation will increase competition for plum job assignments and opportunities.

Managing People Who Are Older Than You

■ *Those in the so-called Generation X sometimes complain of the difficulty in managing those who are older than themselves. What advice would you give them?*

Much of it comes down to a difference in perception about

styles and priorities of management. Young managers should begin by spending time getting to know these older colleagues. While some may view this as unnecessary socialization, not doing so can be the critical disconnect between older workers and a younger supervisor. Even dedicating an hour of time to each individual will demonstrate to him or her that the manager appreciates that person's experience and value.

But this is not where the effort should end. Continue by keeping these people in the loop. Ask them what they think. Solicit their insights on all manner of issues. Chances are, these workforce veterans possess some native knowledge about certain situations that could be very useful. Successful leaders know that seeking the ideas of subordinates enhances, not detracts from, their power and influence. If these individuals like or admire the supervisor, they will share not only insights that might be obvious but also the nuances of navigating company politics.

Job Expectations

■ *Many veteran supervisors express concern about the significantly different job expectations of younger generations. How do you explain these differences?*

Many of these differences can be attributed to three factors: media influence, societal expectations, and the natural impatience of youth. Generation X and especially the Millennials have come of age being fed a constant diet of stories about what work should be like: exciting, stimulating, and fun. They've seen certain occupations dramatized and glamorized in television shows. Many have come to believe that if their job is not as interesting as what they see on TV, they must be in the wrong position.

Then there are societal expectations. Corporate leaders have been lionized in the media over the past fifteen years. They have witnessed the creation of the celebrity CEOs. They begin to think to themselves, "Why not me?" Then they go to work and find themselves enduring the mundane and repetitive work that exists in the majority of occupations.

Finally, there is the natural impatience of youth. Many young people long to be in charge from the moment they step into the workplace. Sometimes peer or parental pressures to succeed exacerbate this desire. But with the confluence of these three factors, it's no wonder that young workers become restless at an earlier time than their older counterparts.

Is there a way to address these differences? Yes, but there are no quick fixes. The first step is to find ways to engage these young people in what they're doing. How do they fit in? Why does the seemingly boring job they do make a difference? How can they begin to collect the experiences and learn the skills that will serve them later on? How can they find mentors and advisers who can provide the invaluable wisdom they will not receive from classroom learning? Addressing these issues and the concerns they express is a great way to build their engagement and productivity.

Communication Styles

■ *Younger generations seem more detached in their communication styles. What impact is this having on the workplace? How should employers deal with these differences effectively?*

A great deal of the differences among communication styles can be attributed to the evolution of electronic technology. As Generation X and especially the Millennials have come of age, they have been immersed in an environment that allows them to communicate in ways to which older generations did not have access. The upside of this is that it can allow for more efficient communication. The downside is that the nonverbal parts of communication have been removed. While older generations have taken note of this phenomenon, younger generations don't see a real difference. This manifests itself in the workplace when someone in his fifties, for instance, prefers to call on the phone, and his younger counterpart favors e-mail. It irritates both of them and impacts productivity.

Contributing to this challenge are those who choose to screen all their calls using voice mail, pagers, and e-mail. While this is far from a generational phenomenon, it has taught those new to the workforce that this practice is acceptable.

As for dealing with these challenges, employers need to understand that this is not a passing phenomenon. Younger generations will continue to drive these changes as time goes on. One of the best ways to address this is to encourage the generations to dialog about how these differences might be better handled. Bring it up at meetings. Pose case studies about typical communication disconnects. Make sure it's out in the open. But this is an evolutionary process that will require constant vigilance.

Views on Training and Development

■ *The generations seem to have different views of the roles, uses, and acquisition of training and education. How do you explain these different views?*

Matures and Boomers share similar views that the training provided should be contributing to the organization's goals. After all, you are learning on company time. These two generations have always taken the long view, believing that training is a path to promotion and additional compensation.

Gen Xers, however, take a more entrepreneurial attitude. They view training and development as a means for enhancing their versatility in the marketplace—as an investment in their future with any employer, not just the present organizaton. Some may protest that Gen Xers have an obligation to remain with the organization where the training was provided. But Xers will retort that a job is a contract and the onus is on the organization to keep them engaged and growing. If not, all bets are off.

Most Millennials have only progressed as far as entry-level skill training at this point in time. Few have matured enough to have experienced the more advanced training they will receive over time. But we suspect that they will treat the acquisition of skills and training in much the same way as their older brethren, the Gen Xers. As Xers assume more and more leadership responsibility, they will probably reinforce this understanding.

Adaptation to and Use of Electronic Technology

■ *The younger a person is, the more he or she seems to embrace electronic technology. How do different generations view the role of these devices in their lives and in the workplace?*

As electronic technology has evolved over the past forty years, each successive generation has become more dependent on it in its daily life. Matures grew up with telephone operators or secretaries who placed their calls, for instance. The Baby Boomers grew up with dial telephones. Xers grew up with cordless phones, and Millennials are growing up with wireless communications.

The big difference in adaptation seems to be the level of immersion and dependence for each generation. The Matures and Boomers came of age in an era when most chores in everyday life were done manually. They, of course, strived to invent new technology that would provide both efficiency and convenience. Gen Xers and the Millennials both adapted to these technologies as children and improved them over time.

But technology is a mixed blessing. While we are now able to produce letters in half the time, we're also finding that many young people have failed to learn proper grammar and composition. So while electronic technology has improved workplace efficiency for some tasks, it has negated efficiency for others. There's nothing wrong with technology itself. We just have to understand the dependence it creates in young people and the impact of this dependence in the workplace.

Views on Money

■ *The generations seem to have wildly differing views on earning, spending, and saving money. How do you reconcile these differences?*

Matures grew up learning that "a penny saved is a penny earned" and that you needed to "put something away for a rainy day." Even in their old age, they remain conservative spenders, opting to do without rather than spending impulsively.

Many Baby Boomers have followed the antithesis of this approach. Over the years the members of this generation have racked up enough consumer debt to seriously endanger their ability to retire in a timely fashion. Baby Boomers were the first credit-card generation. Unfortunately, many have not learned the devastating power behind the time-value of money, leaving them with debts they will be forced to pay down in their later years. This, of course, has made many rethink their goals about working.

Generation Xers, having come of age after the chaos of the sixties and seventies, coupled with watching their parents spend extravagantly, have chosen the more conservative paths of saving and spending prudently. The Millennials, on the other hand, are displaying spending habits remarkably similar to the Baby Boomers, having come of age in the era of credit cards rather than cash. While many of them have learned to spend substantial amounts of money at an earlier age than previous generations, their attitudes about spending in general are viewed as troubling by many.

Rewards and Compensation

■ *Different generations seem to possess different beliefs about the rewards that a job should provide. How do you reconcile these differences?*

This all comes down to what each age group seeks in return for its time and effort. Matures come from an era that taught them duty to country and community. They have applied these values to the workplace as well. Matures feel rewarded by a job well done. While they, like everyone else, want to be well compensated, they take pride in what they have accomplished. Boomers certainly take pride in their work, but they also derive their rewards from the recognition for their contributions to the organization.

Because those in Generation X tend to look at a job as more of a contract, they apply more practicality to the rewards. First, they expect fair compensation and the opportunity to earn extra for doing extra. Second, they seek opportunities to build skills and credentials that will help position them for the future. Third, they value time off, which will provide the balance they seek. Finally, they look for an enjoyable atmosphere where work is not taken too seriously.

As the leading edge of the Millennials has entered the workforce, employers have discovered that "fun" and "stimulation" seem to be the operative words for rewarding this generation. Employers embracing these desires have been able to maintain lower turnover rates and higher productivity. While Millennials know they have to work, they will do so more effectively if they are having fun and feel some control over their environment.

Providing Coaching and Feedback

■ *It's obvious that each generation desires a different type of feedback. How can a manager best provide this, especially when there are four generations in the workplace?*

Matures tend to perform best with clear direction and reinforcement for doing a good job. Coaching, as we know it today, is somewhat of an anomaly to them. While they believe it can have value, they view it as more of a Baby Boomer invention than a critical part of the supervisory process.

Some Baby Boomers have embraced the concept of business coaching wholeheartedly, attending clinics and earning certifications. Others view it with skepticism, wondering whether it is one more passing fad. How they might respond to a supervisor using these coaching techniques depends upon how they interpret the whole concept.

As one might expect, the members of Generation X are skeptical of coaching, first because it seems to be a Boomer invention, and second because they typically enjoy a more hands-off supervisory style. They're apt to think, "If you want to apply coaching techniques, that's fine. Just don't get in my way while I'm getting the job done."

The jury is still out on Millennials since most are still

in jobs that require direct supervision. While some managers may attempt to apply coaching techniques, this may prove ineffective in the entry-level positions Millennials now fill. As they matriculate into the professional workforce, they may embrace these concepts because they have similar beliefs about teamwork to those of their parents, the Boomers.

Index

"Baby Boom," origin of term, 123

Baby Boomers
  as big spenders, 135
  career development, 127
  and coaching, 137
  and compensation, 136
  and credit cards, 135
  demographics, 123–124
  and education, 132
  and electronic technology, 133–134
  as first credit-card generation, 135
  and training, 132
  work ethic, 125–126
  work/life balance, 126–127

Bolles, Richard, 127

Clurman, Ann, 123
coaching, 137–138
communication style, 131–132

compensation, 135–136
Copeland, Douglas, 124

decision making, speed of, 103

Echo Boomers, 124
education, 132–133
electronic technology
  generational differences, 104, 133–134
  as investment in marketability, 104
e-mail, generational differences in use of, 131

feedback, 137–138

generations, grouping of, 123–124
Generation WHY, 124
Generation X, 124

Generation Xers
  career development, 128
  and compensation, 136
  demographics, 124
  and education, 132
  and electronic technology,
    134
  entrepreneurial attitudes,
    132
  job expectations, 129–130
  managing older workers,
    128–129
  nonverbal communication
    style, 131
  origin of term, 124
  as prudent spenders, 135
  skeptical of coaching, 137
  skepticism of, 120
  and training, 132
  work ethic, 126
  work/life balance, 127
Generation Y, 124
G.I.s, 123
Great Expectations, 123

Howe, Neil, 124

impatience of youth, effect on
  job expectations, 130

job expectations, generational
  differences, 129–130
Jones, Landon, 123

Matures
  career development, 127
  and coaching, 137
  coining of term, 123
  and compensation, 136
  as conservative spenders, 134
  demographics, 123
  and education, 132
  and electronic technology,
    133–134
  preference for verbal com-
    munication, 131
  and training, 132
  work ethic, 125
  work/life balance, 126
media influence, on job expectations, 129–130
Millennials
  as big spenders, 135
  career development, 128
  and coaching, 137–138
  and compensation, 136
  demographics, 124
  and electronic technology,
    134

job expectations, 130
nonverbal communication
style, 131
work ethic, 126
"working the system," 120
work/life balance, 127
money, generational differences, 134–135

Net-Geners, 124
Nexters, 124, *see also*
Millennials

older workers, *see also* Matures
acceptance of, 103
attitude toward younger
workers, 105
balancing past *vs.* future,
103
being stuck in a rut, 109
generalizing about, 106
management of, 128–129
resistance to change, 108

rewards, generational differences, 135–136
Rocking the Ages, 123
role perception, as guide to
behavior, 108–109

saving, generational differences, 134–135
Silents, *see* Matures
Smith, Walker, 123
societal expectations, effect
on job expectations,
130
spending, generational differences, 134–135
Strauss, William, 124

technology, *see* electronic technology
training, 132–133

Veterans, 123

What Color Is Your Parachute?,
127
work ethic, generational differences, 125–126
workplace
creating the right environment, 119, 120
differences in work ethic,
119, 125–126

younger workers, *see also*
Millennials

younger workers, *cont.*
  accepting advice of older
    workers, 108
  ambition of, 106
  exuberance of, 106
  impatience of, 106–107, 130
  need for mentors, 130
  need for reflection, 108
  need to be taken seriously,
    107
  seeking perspective of oth-
    ers, 105

About the Authors

ROBERT W. WENDOVER is Managing Director of The Center for Generational Studies, a sociological research firm based in Aurora, Colorado. He is the author of *Hey Dude! The Manager's Short Course on the Emerging Generations* and *Generations: Understanding Age Diversity in Today's Workplace* among other publications. A frequent guest on radio and television, he has been writing and speaking on age diversity for more than a decade. He lives in Centennial, Colorado.

TERRENCE GARGIULO is an international speaker, author, organizational development consultant, and group process facilitator. He holds a Master of Management in Human Services from the Florence Heller School at Brandeis University and is a recipient of *Inc.* magazine's Marketing Master Award. Some of his past and present clients include GM, DTE Energy, Dreyers Ice Cream, UnumProvident, the U.S. Coast Guard, Boston University, Raytheon, the city of Lowell, Massachusetts, Arthur D. Little, KANA Software, Merck-Medco, Coca-Cola, Harvard Business School, and Cambridge Savings Bank. The opera *Tryillias*, written by Terrence and his father, was accepted for nomination for a Pulitzer Prize in music in 2004. Terrence resides in Monterey, California, with his wife and son, and is an avid scuba diver, passionate chef, and lyric baritone.

ELDON DEDINI is an award-winning cartoonist and illustrator whose work has appeared in many national publications, including *The New Yorker, Playboy,* and *Esquire* magazines. His work has also appeared in several cartoon anthologies and in books by Max Schulman, Art Buchwald, and others. He is the author of *The Dedini Gallery* (1961) and *A Much, Much Better World* (1985). Mr. Dedini is a four-time winner of the Best Magazine Cartoonist award from the National Cartoonists Society. He lives in Monterey, California.

FOR MORE INFORMATION

Be sure to visit the book's website for additional materials and information:

http://www.OnCloudNine.org

ROBERT WENDOVER
rwendover@OnCloudNine.org

TERRENCE GARGIULO
tgargiulo@OnCloudNine.org

In-depth information on generational challenges in the workplace can be found at:

CENTER FOR GENERATIONAL STUDIES
http://www.gentrends.com
Phone: 800-227-5510

In-depth information on how to leverage the power of stories can be found at:

MAKINGSTORIES.net
http://www.MAKINGSTORIES.net
Phone: 781-894-4381